Looking for Jonathan

Looking for
Jonathan

Jon Anderson

University of Pittsburgh
Press

811
An23l

Some of these poems appeared in *Badlands Review Defunct, Choice, Dickinson Review, Fall River Review, Hudson Review, Kayak, North American Review, Poetry Northwest, Tri-Quarterly,* and the anthologies *Midland 2* (Dial Press) and *The Young American Poets* (Follett Publishing Company). "The Monument to Resignation" and "Looking for Jonathan" first appeared in *Poetry.* The first two lines of part v of "The Summer Deaths" are from John Ashbery's poem "The Picture of Little J. A. in a Prospect of Flowers," included in his book *Some Trees,* published by Yale University Press.

The epigraph to this book is from the author's memory of the Francois Truffaut and Jean Gruault film *Jules and Jim,* which is based on the novel by Henri-Pierre Roché.

These poems would not have been possible without the assistance and inspiration of Marvin Bell, Joseph de Roche, and David Schloss. Particular thanks go to George Starbuck for his advice and patience.

*for my mother and father
and Victoria and Julla*

Contents

Jim would have liked their ashes to be mingled; Catherine, to have hers scattered to the winds. But it was not permitted.

—Jules and Jim

Dear Anyone:

It Is Morning; the Animals

It is morning; the animals
have come back, awake, amid seasons
of themselves. Walking under the arced boughs
and the moon, they have remembered
the dream they are living now,
and yesterday, and when the water
became more subtle, into marsh, and then land.
They come with only a little caution,
the lizard extending his tongue
into the sunlight, zebras
becoming blond, the raccoon
reaching into newness, toward death.
One pale lion turns on its back,
dreaming in the grass which is bloodied
and bright. In his dream he says: *My friend.*

And it is true. Each animal
stands in its green contemplative room,
even in blood, in daylight to the ears,
saying: *My friend. Be calm.*
You are forgiven, even
unto death. The lion
places his soft paw
on the shoulder of a man:
This is my peaceable son;
my fond intention, dreaming,
even unto death. The sun blazes.

The animals lie down.
Everywhere the ground trembles

with their muscular sleep.
The man disappears, as though
he was not ever in that house at all,
but was invisible, or asleep
deep in the lion's dark belly,
or was the lion, dreaming of him.

Abraham

Westward, our recluse neighbor
has fired his crops
against disease. The landscape
sways, a lake of flame.

In the red summer
we rise and dress in the dark,
we lift the latch
on brightness, walk

down to the stricken lovers
scattered this side of the river.
Everywhere hands touch,
wheat cracks, cornstalks

are torches,
wildflowers
rock in their vases of flame.
Deep in his own thought

the neighbor smiles:
now the land's not his,
nor was,
nor will become

anything more than his love burned down.
His million sons
whirl westward, dressed
in the curling sacrificial gowns.

Odalisque

Vacuuming naked
this morning, balancing
on her puffed, white stomach

the silver head of a dog
(a chained medallion),
she whispers desperately.

The cold coin rises
consciously taking her breath,
the morning,

right out of her lungs.
Eyes, red obsidian
and black,

leap at her face
& the jaw snaps back
against her left breast

and her heart.
Is she whispering: *Love me?*
The child

in her belly awakens, turns:
Countess, Lover,
here I am,

dangling from my watch chain.
Over the sly
wheeze of the machine

it sucks at her heart,
blindly, as if in love.
Both of them dream then, awake.

The dog's head
swings on its chain
forward & back,

a cold hand on her chest,
and pushing its legs
deep within her thighs,

the child walks.

The Young Wife

i

Holding our hands to the light,
we saw wings beating
the blood in the wrists.
A man's hand relaxes
into a cup, a woman's
reaches toward the man's,
or what he was reaching for,
which is nearer her. Turned
off the lights, over
the bed, & everywhere.

ii

Nights when it rains in the midwest
it means different things: how steel rails
flash momentarily behind the last sleeping-car,
or to a farmer, listening in the night,
if this kind of solitude is worth it.

iii

If I appeared to have fallen into doubt,
or to have taken myself seriously—
that's all right. I seemed to be dying there.
Not alone, really, but out of sight, which
is the same thing, only smaller.

iv
I have a name sewn to my scarf—
that's like saying who I am.
Unspoken, it could be "Knowledge"
or "Bad Dream." Whenever
you speak to me, I am still
young enough to be surprised.
Which is like saying there are
promises I cannot keep.

On a Rainy Night, an Ape in Scarsdale, N.Y., Returns a Library Book

for Robert Bly

He pulls his car
under the running, street-lit leaves.
2 A.M.
The dashlight reddens his jaw;
and his eyes, like thunder,
disappear. Or I think that

about apes. Gets out. & slams the door.

Hand & hand, over the olive lawn—
Will his wife, in New Jersey, worry?
—About the lateness of the hour?
—The dark invitation of trees
lining roads all the way home?
The lawn sighs
beneath his weight. Damp circles start
under his elbows and knees.
At a darkened doorway, he stops:
he cools his head on a stone.

A book
whistles down the chute.
That's all?

Back over the lawn,
the trees look down, the moon
frankly looks at this. Low moans
circle his sweaty head
& fly away. What if he sang?

Robt., I mean this:

He carried the moon
like a book beneath his left arm.
And before we could speak:

He drives away.

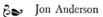

The Frontier

for Jim Tate

When I ask for Lao Tzu
it's you.

The Masked Ball
to which everyone came dressed
as a telephone. No one

was left to answer.
That was the weekend of

The Continual Celebration of Retrospect.

Mother,
Homecoming, the best
of the Big Ten, the Illustrated
Index to Pound's Cantos.

But you were the loneliest poet alive.

That is: the old Chinese lawbreaker
facing the lavish weather
at Land's End.

Aviators

We learned, and slowly, only
that we fell in the high spiral

of confusion. The millionth run—
and now our lives unwound.

Well, we had always had bright flak at heart.
And when we stalled our bomber under

the new moon, and emerged—who could have known?
In that musical dangle, jukebox angels

fed us their sweet compassionate bread.
Our bellies grew round as the red moon,

and we starved. Who could survive
desire? They have wired

our wild hearts for sound. We are falling down
forever toward your blue receding town.

The Miracle

The Altitudes. Aerial act,
circa 1910:
they fly by, odd moths, green,

eyes as blue
as the rare air
they exhale. You knew

Pa-pa, a legend
in organdy tights.
He made the rose-lights

lithe, to follow
the arc he swung.
The silk air bagged in his lungs.

When the first shock struck
he was high;
then the dark

above his head
grew large—and he was cold,
an old man, balanced in the light.

He clings—
The crowd screams—
But he shows them the ten

tiny glass angels
in his hands.
These flicker. He falls,

years, into their arms.
They are reaching upward,
as if alone.

The night winds
trouble them. The galaxies
turn in their hands.

Fox

Fox, eyes red,
stands on the rocks.

Puts his long head
down to the lake,

drinks cold oil.
Overhead

the jets wheel & go to sea.
Fox is thoughtful,

an indifferent ear.
If he listens, he hears

Wing Commander Joe
shift in the dark electronics.

Nijinski, the wind
whispers

on the wings,
Where are you now,

the radar sings.

World War II

Now the soldiers
grow shorter, marching

into their mothers' wombs.
Korea sleeps.

The Thresher turns on its side.
Many sailors have come home

unrecognizably older.
In the arctic, Nansen

still eats soup.
Under his fire

the ice clears to glass.
He trusts himself.

If I Had It To Do Again

Of the bloody palate,
who is it?
Robierre, boy
without fame, dishwasher. Poet,

who cracks the cups
in the restaurant's steel sink.
Who bites
his tongue raw, for spite.

The hours are piling into his head.
He's not thinking about it.
The editors
are insulting each other outside his door.
So he's not there . . .

Meanwhile downtown he's meeting one friend
and another.
He carries his jacket
like a sleeping Negro
over his shoulder.
Hiya, hiya, says the first friend, hiya,
says the other.

Shall I tell you about him?
  He reads the poetry of friends without envy.
  He's maybe not a fairy, but he can touch
        a man's arm with no embarrassment.
  His women are loved without promises.
    But all the while he's looking them in the eye, and
    he can let his penis sleep in a widow's hand.

You made a fool out of him?
He never knew it.

So here we are again,
  reading each other's verse
  in the high, believable grass.

"Robierre," I say,
"If you gave it all up . . . "

  He agrees.
            Robierre,
boy dishwasher,
poet without fame.

Not Loves, I Think, But Shapes
They Leave Behind

You remember how it was:
She was always alone.
   (Her one small room. Remember?)
And she was always in.
And she was always kind to us,
who cared for her.

Still, she would sometimes cry.
You remember, how she cried their names:
that high, small sound
   (you said like birds).
Your father and I
would carry her through all the rooms.
And she would count the rooms

and listen (I wondered what she heard)
and take their objects up.
Vases, figurines. Her hands
turning over each dear shape
   (you wondered what she found)
and how her hands
would simulate each shape
after she had placed it down.

Benedicite

Sir, here on my table
is a miracle:
two cups, white
upon the white folds
of the cloth, and milk,
and breakfast rolls.
These we had planned,
and have survived
our mortal sleep.
Behind you the window
opens outward;
light sits upon
your shoulder
like the Morning Angel:
round and vigilant.
Though we are private,
temporary things
we will, this once,
take milk and bread
and be companions of
a common table.
Then if our animal hearts
desire it, we may,
like clear water
over stones, go outward
into a meeting with
the formal shapes of day.

The Summer Deaths:

Entrance to a Mirror

This is a still life,
shade beneath which

configurations
come forward to you.

I am coming
toward you. The deep

chairs, the piano
and thin glass vases

darken behind me,
coming to the door.

Here is evening, here
are white roses and

my hand. The windows
stand very straight, as

if amazed, but are
closing now against

us and the light. Here
is your glass hand. In

our faces, roses
like whitened wax, shine.

The Murderer, for Love's Sake, Relents

It is your russet throat
of which I speak, not
horses, whole furred teams,
their snapped reins streaming
as they run by, shouting;

Nor baboons, but your red
arched throat & the blue veins
lining it, which push my love,
hotly, out of the breasts I
touch, up into your clear head,

Bringing me now toward
balance, your delightful head
balanced above your breasts
and, beneath, your legs
striding confidently forward

Into my vision, a country
of tall horses, kneeling
among the long spines
of the grasses, but ready,
my love, to stand calmly

Should baboons with blue hearts
step out of our whole lives,
bow, and ride steadily
away, the dark hooves beating
wherever I touch your breasts.

Paris

Lying beside you
I was hurt

by the lightness
of your breath.

Will you die?
I think of Paris, where

it is beginning
to be morning: Boys

ride bicycles
over the wet streets,

a slow trail warms, evaporates . . .
I will be homeless again.

The Summer Deaths

i
The year we
came upon
the fox's skull
I think that
I was still
in love with
life. Then, that
peculiar
fragrance of
the calm bone
thrilled, until
the very
dolphins of
the airy
summer light
dipped, nuzzled
us with love
of . . . what? Death?
We survived.
Dark angels,
like the leaves'
soft shadows
rubbed our hearts.
But no one died.

ii

What was your name? You
were my first love at
the summer lake. That
year the cold blue
waters brought me up,
lean and wet, into
your first, hard kiss. Oh,
you were perverse! But

I buried my face
in your crisp black hair,
tongued the dampness there,
and your wild heart raced.

And you were better
than a boy! You came
apart. And the same
feminine rage tore

in me when we lay
down. Ah, my sweet
bitch, you ripped my heart,
but I took yours away.

iii

Christ, I was twelve
when I gave up my love
to you & burned in your streaming
wounds. I was the skinniest
kid in camp; I dreamed;
I faithfully wet
my bed. Only your wilderness,
berries and nuts, red
bushes gone to flame,
kept me apart
from each ordered day.
For one whole month
(August) I imagined your delicate
hands, your red mouth
pushing at my flesh. But,
in truth, it was your marvelous,
intricate pain that was temptation.
My dear Christ,
how often you came at night
redeeming some of us
(who *knew*)
from the counselor's planned salvations.
How I loved you.
Out of the dark your pale, intense
teenager's face
swayed behind our tent.
O, I'm here, come out, I'm here . . .
Whatever we learned
we learned through our disgrace
at being twelve, and not yet
willing to tear at
our loins, or to burn
in our private, downy hair
for love of you.

iv

Dimaggio, Pesky,
Williams, Stephens, Doerr,
Goodman, Zarilla,
Tebbetts, Parnell or

Kinder: men, you lost
it all by just one game.
One! Damn! One! Every
year it was the same

bad story. Fly balls
to the fence. And sweat.
The long slide into
third. The easy out.

And the seasons slipped,
like us, from the park.
O the pale snow soars,
soars in the outfield dark.

V

In a far recess of summer
monks are playing soccer.

Between the damp leaves
we can barely hear their calls

coming, or the soft leather
punt of the ball. But I'd rather

not remember. Their distant
passionless cries were hesitant

in the trees. I kissed
the book I read. I caressed

the smooth defenseless underside of
your arm. Another love,

I have put you away
in the safety of the way

those far monks joyously cried,
and you are foreign at my side.

The Well

And as I leaned,
desiring to step forever
down, or drown
heavily, a whole man
dropping into
the hall of water,
I said a name (though
I had meant it to be
your own).
Half of the light
fled backward then,

and half of the name
tumbled bodily
between the deep
blue moss and stone,
darkening there.

Hatless, some of me
foolish, or alone,
I turned (as you
would have turned
had you been there)
back to the year's
bad poems, one
temperate girl
I had betrayed in pain,
and all of the hurt
world, into whose secret
pitying ear
I had said my name.

The Angel of Departures

Continents watch through windows.
The lovers sleep, the trees
lean into their shadows.
Coming between stars,
the eye of the angel rises.
He is boyish, shy.

Illusionless, the earth
reverses beneath his stare;
the seas shine—but briefly.
Though even the deepest
waters have exchanged,
it is in a decent dream.

Now the lovers awaken
into a clear morning.
They appear to be touching.
We watch them walk
beneath the changed, black
boughs, the sons you will
never sustain, the poems
I will not begin again.

Death's Only Son

I wanted to be
brilliant glass, worn
at my throat.

Whoever I faced
would become clear to me.
I wanted to be Death's

only son, the favorite,
constantly refused.
Ritual, our bond.

I stand among friends,
representing them;
their flesh, like

damp bread, softens.
Now I am lonely.
And when they turn,

their mouths small
and old, I think
it is to speak of me.

Memory, we grow
restless, you & I,
and accidental.

The Blue Animals

When I awoke this morning
they were there, just as blue
as the morning, as calm
as the long green lawn

they grazed upon, turning
their delicate heads. You
would have said: No harm
shall befall us. But you were gone.

So these two opened my morning
gracefully wide and blue
as the morning sky. Their calm
mouths moved over the lawn,

and as I was turning
to call out again for you,
I saw there was no harm
at all, though you were gone.

Milkweed

Bitch, today I
rummaged in a picture book,
horny for myself.

One word got through: Excuse.
A few of the rest
crawled away blind, & hid.

So when I gave up
& jacked off
(not without delicacy

or thoughts of you), those
incomprehensible remainders
like ticks & beetles

walked under the bed.
Then came, whispering
to lunch: I mean

meanings
in the sweet, pale milk.
Marry me, we

can abuse each other
skillfully. We
can beat our kids

black & starry with love
until, like white
hairs or

parachutes, their tiny
silken cries
fill up the night.

Preparation for Travel

for Linda

Someone has lost a note from his mother.
Another has bad wings.
Also Reader I hope
you are home and between cool linens.

For although
the door opens, no one comes in.
        I am locked in a house
where everyone flies up.
    One by one God is removing us
    (pray for us).
His large head, like a horned
owl's, comes between the trees,

and I believe he is coming here.
    So that I hug my knees, learning
    solicitude:
                to watch my wrist-watch, like
                a silkworm, spin.

The fortunate man sleeps—
    and his dream goes over the gates, gathering
speed, by dried ponds, lawns,
the constant headlights, and
        more peaceable homes.

When at last it rests,
            it is a sheet over the sea.

The angel also goes by,
coming here.
                And we, here,
outside the asylum's gate, are packing,
although there is no solution.

I hear the angel speak,
kindly,
but we are denied companions.

    For my birthday
God gave me 10,000 white birds, so that I
        would not be alone, but I am.
So I am writing to you,
the only poem I ever write; badly,
but in sincerity.
    I am trying to love you.
Love me. I have no shame.

The New World

It was your own
pain, brilliant
oil at the lips of the very young, and
freaking out,
you spilled your hurt flesh
on my shirt—a personal
night.

X,
my fabulous teenage mistress,
whenever you fight the cops
I hide, like a soft dog
on the wall. Though I

would lick your red brain
clean, and your pain.

Sledding over the million brilliant
particles of snow,
I can bring you back
again, but not
to anyone. So I took home

your almond hand
& your hair, streaming
over my opposite shoulder.

At dinner our friends smiled,
spoke of us softly.
Though both of us feared
the footfalls of wolves, black
shapes on the distant snow, it was

the adamant journey,
the New World,
too distant to see clearly . . .

The Happiest Man:

It's me again. Nights
I lie, hot,
under the electric light,

deep in my own soup.
The personal red radio
I am desiring

beats back: "Hello
Lover." Home again:
the anxious angel,

wings in my darkest bowel.
That's Jonathan's bed,
singing. I'm thinking

maybe it's the mad
who circle up the bedsprings;
or the dead

are really here, signaling.
For the sake of
no one, I'm still awake,

hearing the filaments sing.
And no one is here
under the angel's wing, his

irrelevant tongue in my ear.

Voyage

for Joseph

So, at last, we *will* cross.
Our season presupposes continents, lands
of desire. We toss
like unloved baggage where we stand,

and slowly the land gives over.
Good-bye; good-bye.
The water
rises and hisses; distance simplifies

trees, houses. The small land speeds.
And we escape.

Here is your flying sea,
proportionless, your seascape

hung with birds, your frail launch
lightly bearing us in mist.
Everything's touch;
immediate. We had this

journeying at heart; yes, days
of it, weeks, bouyant, propelled.
The casual waves
blur like lines cast back. We have ourselves

out here; what else?
Birds fail. The sea shines
daily, is calm and—who can tell?—
bottomless. There will be time.

And here I awakened into fear—
a destination, as your own;
an inlet, where
the waters shine

in welcome, where the journey
cries out: *Here,* where stones, enormous,
burrow in the sea.
The shoreline grows,

specific, black and real.
Here is your consummate island;
mine. The sea is still.
The launch glides inland.

We stand in this full calm,
a journey's
end. Friend, be kind,
foreshadow me.

Song of the Refugee

I found, in my own room:
an open drawer, piety
on my key chain, thoughts
without hair. I
was an eye that looked away.

I put my head
on my bald
chest. (I was an egg!)

That was the end
of kidding myself.
                    But later
notes from former
friends were pinned to the walls,
locks of their longest hair,
greetings for every season.

Convalescence,
with my bags
locked in his wagon, looked in.
I was eating my second supper.
I said: Brother,
But for you
look what they'd have forgotten.

He couldn't be fooled.

He sold everything: rings,
silver, my Portable Rilke;

he gnawed holes
in my brightest clothes,
barked at the postman, and
moved in.

I wanted to be
the man who remembered everyone,
the biggest cathedral,

and here I am, the confessor.

Totem

In a pitched bed. I
am pink, in love with
heat. Out in the afternoon
a red barn shifts, turns
down Beacon Street.

I am gliding amidst
foghorns and in a dream.
Oars lock in my high
secretive skull; I
drift between doors
into the flooded dark.
Here is the home
of nighthawks and owls.
A massive protection
opens in my head—
indoor afternoons:
the house smelled of
dampness, the shadow
of the piano reached
across the living
room. *Mom's
gone upstairs.* Now

the echo of water
knocks about, the odor
of pine-pitch and cedar
lolls all over. Stripped
to the waist, I touch
for the snouts of seals

in the dark. Somewhere
trees are bending in
an afternoon; also my
face, sticky as a leaf bud,
opens. I am truly tired.
My mother mentions me.
Two or three times, I
am arriving home.

The Implantation

He believed his childhood lay outside himself

Mother, you touch me.
Then I misunderstand.
The pale, rubber doll
you offer grows waxlike
& warm, and enters,
like a foreign child,
my side. My new rib
circles the moon—
phlegm rises within
my chest—white feathers
of pollen, a swan—

    Rachel!
            Your furious child

hammers beneath my heart!
When I bend, demurely
as the neck of a swan,
it is into the blade
of daylight, or (over
& over) my mother's arm.

    January:
    I lightened. I bled
    when the sled's blade
    cut my flesh.
    Father encircled it.
    My mother, Frances
    Elizabeth, touched the red wrist
    to her lips. For this

I would save buttons, bottled string,
implements, peach pits, hairs of the dead
wizened child I was (for how
        could he then die
for lack of the gathered world?
        or anyone die?)
        Not this year.
        The gold leaves
        redden the square;
        the weather cools.
        In my chest
        the curled fist loosens. For this

I would illuminate your house,
my mother, wife, protectress, temptress,

        giving you grief & sons.

53

Self-Portrait as a Sparrow

In his room,
alone, he hears
within his head
a music for harpsichord:
the intelligence
of birds, of
sparrows. His eye cocks.
Lost in the upper
branches, surrounded
and shadowed by leaves,
he feels his
high house weave
in the wind; his
world bends
everywhere. And he
has come to know
these northern winds,
even by sound alone.

Now frail bones
toss in the wind as
he races toward town—
small-voiced
and whimsical,
the ecstatic bearer
of false alarms.

The Monument to Resignation

Then I was crazy,
wearing my solitude lightly—
the colored duck

breeding war in a thatched hut—
but I couldn't have loved you less.

I washed my weapons in
the day's events; went out,
armed, at night.

My door
opened on the new unknown.
I threw stones

at the houses of starlets,
then ran off, colorless,
into the shadows.

But the danger wouldn't disappear.
No one would let me in.
My house
was a column of salt.

So I left, living
for years on water and grain.

And one spring morning
I passed by and
laid this poem, like an ordinary head,
on my old doorstep.

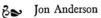

The Dream of Compassion

for Steve Orlen

The man turns toward me.
I say: Everything
will arrive, or I take

his grown face
in my hands.

Leaving in pieces, I am
going home now.

My terror, the white compassion
pushes against my sides;
my wrists
rise into the soft snow

which is falling.
The man
retreats; the darkness
takes my shape.

Then it's late.
It was too close to dreaming.
Even as I returned that look
I was dying

three, or four ways at once.
And the last
was precious, was turning away.

In my sleep, the shadow
of a storm. It moves

easily in.
The man,
who does not dream

mightily, curls
for the journey in my right arm.

The River

At the Film Institute
they were showing
STEPHEN DAVID JONATHAN JON:
A STORY OF FRIENDS.

In light shells
they fled to where the water seemed to be still.
At every oar, the shadow
dips,
streams, follows after.
                          Toward noon
the sun is a gold drum, beating.
The fields alongside open . . .

for which a man might cry,
for joy. They throw
him overboard. Someone says: O.K.
Who needs to be told?
It's like new silver, the discovery
of a natural system: Water.

At the film's end you are awakened in bed.
Knowledge has put itself
forward in your hand: pictures, blood,
money, the round evidence of
weathers in a tree: Memory.
The nurse takes it away.

Tomorrow,
will it be clear and fabulous?
The meaning might be
dry land.
But you say: *Am I
my own concubine!* Then,
milder: *Was it really here?*
Too late. The past,
who knew you, has retreated.

Meanwhile, *Eat,* say the days.
*Drink. Of yourself,
the river. Sleep,
in silver obedience, like the water.*

The History of Psychotherapy

I find many dishes
lie on the dark lawn, waiting.

Now for the history of love:

A man found a locket
—or amulet—
anyway, a real disc, cold
silver in his bed.
He opened it.
Much of the rest

is an underground journey, soft noses
   of moles,
running water,
the occasional
distant emergencies: holding aliens
   or ships, in time of war.

In the end, he might arrive.
His childhoods
surprise him:
                    Thousands
of motionless, small toads.
But each sleeps, for love, in a dish.

The entire scene
is opening.
Clarity, I think I am
coming toward you, I bear
myself with such indifference.

Looking for Jonathan

Before sunrise
the sky whitened. I said
to myself: "Whatever troubles you,
leave it."
      Then we're speeding
into the fields,
   corn, white houses,
buses at daybreak: the same eyes
we've brought along before.

But the yellow light
looked
   in at us: "That discomfiture—
give it here."

O, I knew what
had been planned, but where?
   And in whose name?

Non-Fiction, happiest man, ran alongside,
   then right-angled "See you—"
into the white woods.
   We followed, of course, on foot.

There, various women (some I knew
   or had known) were dancing, filling
a clearing.

      The pond:
We swam in the old way, lit

the green leaves to grow warm.
Our smoke rose into the sun.

When I saw America, she had danced all night,
she was chalk-white,
leaning on her husband's arm.

       I could see
the orange home town, coming.
I leaned honestly
   into my own reflection.
I had no more stories of God.

COLOPHON

The poems in this book were set in Electra, a typeface designed for Linotype by W. A. Dwiggins. The effort was to work into Electra some of the twentieth-century spirit that was developing at the time the face was designed.

The poem titles are set in Weiss, in this instance the Intertype adaption of the Bauer design by Emil Rudolph Weiss.

The display types are Deepdene italics, designed and cut by Frederic W. Goudy in 1927, and named for his estate at Marlboro-on-Hudson. The Monotype recutting, done later, is used here.

The book was printed from the type by Heritage Printers, Inc., on Warren's Olde Style antique wove paper, and bound in Bancroft fabrics. It was designed by Gary Gore.

Pitt Poetry Series